LOVE YOUR LIFE

Love Your Life

▼

A Guide for the Journey

Gayla Y. Rinehart

Writers Club Press
San Jose New York Lincoln Shanghai

Love Your Life
A Guide for the Journey

Writers Club Press
an imprint of iUniverse.com, Inc.

For information address:
iUniverse.com, Inc.
5220 S 16th, Ste. 200
Lincoln, NE 68512
www.iuniverse.com

ISBN: 0-595-14823-9

Printed in the United States of America

This book is dedicated to God. This is His book. I am merely His scribe.

CONTENTS

▼

ACKNOWLEDGEMENTS

▼

First, I would like to thank God for always loving me, guiding me and protecting me in this world. I would like to thank my mother for her love and teaching me as a child about life and about God. My father, even though he is in spirit, is always with me. My daughter Katrina, from whom I experienced growth in myself. My sister Karen, who has always been an encouragement and inspiration. My brothers, Gregg and Glenn, by growing up with them, gave me needed experiences in life.

Great friends who have always been there for me no matter what. Shaharazad for showing me the true meaning of humbleness and humility. Joy for her uplifting support and positive attitude. Susan for making me step beyond my comfort zone. Mirael for setting me onto this path and showing me the way. Robin for keeping me physically fit and spiritually fit. Without their constant unconditional love, encouragement, support and experiences that we have shared and learned from each other along the way, this book may not have been written.

INTRODUCTION

Remembering back to when I was very young, I can remember my mother always explaining and teaching my sister and I all about God and how he loves us and takes care of us. My father died of leukemia at the age of twenty-four when I was six months old. I am sure that through this experience, my mother's firm foundation for belief in God was built and helped serve her through this trying time.

As long as I can remember, my mother always told me the story of how an angel saved my life. It was not long after my father had passed on and I was seven or eight months old. My mother was carrying me in her arms and walking with my sister who was three years old at the time. She was walking down a sidewalk and twisted her ankle. Her fall sent me flying out of her arms and head towards the concrete. My mother fell to the sidewalk and I was miraculously caught by a man dressed in a brown suit. My mother jumped back to her feet and the man in the brown suit handed me back to her arms. She took one look at me and looked up to thank him and he was nowhere to be seen. He had vanished just as quickly as he had appeared.

As I grew up, I realized how many other near misses I was saved from and knew that God wanted me here for a reason and I wanted to find out what my purpose was. What mission had I come to complete?

As a young girl when I started to go to church, I always was in awe and knew that it was a very sacred place since the things my mother taught me were always so special. I have been to many different churches throughout my years, and have studied many different forms of religious faith, and they all have a special sacredness to them.

I started studying different religions on my own and discovered how to put what I had learned into my everyday life. There always seemed to be an answer for every problem. Like everything in life, jobs, relationships, even diets do not work if you do not apply positive energy and conscious effort to it every day. I started listening more to my intuition and connecting with higher levels of consciousness that has kept me focused and determined towards reaching my life goal.

As I noticed the changes happening in my life, I started observing other people's lives and tried to figure out what was making their lives the way they were. I knew what worked and what did not work for me, but what was going on with everybody else?

Can everyone really say that they love their life? I finally came to the realization that our lives are what we make of them. Our life is played out by our conscious direction.

Based on many years working in the healing arts and aesthetic field, in trying to erase the lines of time and worry, I found that the cause of most of these "lines of life" were a result of years of negative thinking and living. Every day we allow into our thoughts what we read in the newspaper, see on the television, and are influenced by our usual daily relations. Everything that we are subjected to in our daily lives is not always particularly positive, and this can make positive thinking and positive living a real challenge.

This book is a powerful tool to help readers focus more towards the positive and achieve balance in their life. This book is spiritually based and focused on our connection with God and how this influences our life. This book will also show how you influence your own life.

This book will address how to identify negativity, fear, doubt and ego situations in your every thought, word and action. You will see that this can all be turned around to allowing the positive to be the controlling factor in your life and through this you can find your Divine plan and love your life.

I have been on my spiritual path for most of my life and have certainly had the experience of what works and what does not work for a happy life. Over the past few years, clients and friends have been volunteering information and having discussions with me as to what makes their life happy or unhappy and I can see it written all over their faces. I have been giving my words of wisdom in which they are grateful and I am starting to see a change in everyone. The writing of this book is spiritually inspired writing. I have been sharing this information and it is helping people look at their lives differently.

I trust these facts will compel you to look at everything in your life and world differently. The way you look at people, yourself, nature...everything that happens in your world. Every single moment is an experience to look at the situation and, in the way you respond to it, forms your world.

Let this information sink into your consciousness and see where it takes you.

Let's Take A Look

▼

Only by nurturing children and protecting
The world we share can we move from the
Century of violence towards lasting peace
-His Holiness the 14th Dalai Lama
Excerpt from Harmony and Diversity

Just the complexity of being born into this world, getting through childhood, and growing up to be a responsible adult with a certain amount of conscious intelligence is a real journey with a lot of lessons along the way. Our journey can be easy, with life being a breeze, or it can be difficult with a lot of sorrow along the way. It is really up to you how you want your life to be. Most people think it is difficult for life to be easy and full of joy, and end up with a life that is easy to be difficult. Our path can be quite easy. We just need the proper tools to make it that way.

When we are born into this world, we are at the mercy of our parents to instill within us certain beliefs, rules, education, knowledge and love. When a child is raised in a loving environment, given certain rules of right and wrong and always encouraged when he or she does well, it makes for a more positive adult with good self-esteem who is therefore successful and happy. As to the contrary, a child raised in an unloving environment with no direction of right or wrong, and without encouragement, makes for an adult with low self-esteem who always feels a failure.

The first five years of a child's life are very impressionable. In a child's efforts to communicate before being able to converse, the child is left with sensing the emotions of the adult. When the child sees or feels disharmony, he or she can sense it and this is recorded in the memory banks, which unfortunately can cause emotional problems as an adult. Children are like tape recorders or sponges: they are recording and absorbing every word that is spoken, any act that is done, any positive or negative emotion that the adult is exhibiting. I can still remember a lot of my mothers conversations when I was young. Children can do this without even looking like they are listening. Everything that they are recording is like a seed being planted and as we know, all seeds grow.

Do you remember as a child, seeing, sensing or feeling what was going on in the room and when it was not harmonious you felt uneasy and unsafe? Adults need to be conscious of the words and actions that are conducting in front of children. We should not say or do anything around children that we would not say to them directly. This is also a point where communication is important since the child will perceive through the adults actions and words something that may not be true. Then go through his or her whole life with a misconception of what the adult had said or done which in turn causes an emotional condition. For instance, a child may think they did something wrong when they see an angry or unhappy expression on an adult's face, when in actuality, the adult was just wearing a look of concern that did not intend to express disapproval. This is why communication is important to let the child know and understand what you are thinking and saying. Children need to be taught to love and be given as much love as possible for this is what they need to pass on to the world as adults. There are a lot of years between birth and adulthood. What happens between these years is the foundation for adulthood and our future experiences: how we look at life and how we form our world.

It is also important not to stifle or discourage children when they have special gifts or interests. Not allowing them to explore their gifts or interests can be harmful, for this is a time when they should be encouraged as much as possible. By expanding their gifts at this point will attune the child to where he or she is comfortable, therefore the child will excel. As a parent, we bring them into this world, but we have no right to keep them from who they are or what they can accomplish. Encouragement and love is positive programming and is a great necessity. Children mainly need to feel safe and loved.

As these children grow into young teenagers, it is a very difficult time, for they are trying to discover themselves and all the previous programming they have had so far comes into play. How they get through this depends on how they are guided by their parents or guardian. Hopefully, this is in a harmonious manner. Disharmony at this point can lead to further emotional problems and lower self-esteem.

When an adult, they are confused and cannot even explain why they have certain issues or hang-ups. These seeds were planted since day one of our birth. Now, maybe you can see why so many people have emotional problems and the *need* for certain chaos in their life. For this is what they grew up with and this is what they know. This is their comfort zone. Continuous love and encouragement are of the utmost importance to children and young adults, and results in a more desirable comfort zone.

Now, on to being an adult. Adulthood is full of love, joy, kindness, compassion, integrity, right? Well, it can be, even if you have had a tough go at life so far. Let us take a look at starting today. Today can be the start at a new way of being, and a new way of living.

To start, we, as humans, have our body that seems to miraculously run on auto-pilot. We do not have to tell our heart to beat, our lungs to breath, or our eyes to see. Our body automatically takes care of us twenty-four hours a day. It reminds us to eat by feeling hungry and to rest by feeling tired. We also store emotions in our body as well as in the mind. For instance, when you are under stress, it can show itself all the way to the skin level. A lot of college students agree that they break out with an acne condition when they are under the stress of getting ready for finals. I have seen this a lot by working in the aesthetic field for many years. Each time I see someone that is complaining of acne, the first question I ask is: "How much stress are you under?" If stress alone can work its way out through your skin, imagine what effect it has had on the internal organs. Emotions do affect the body. As you will see later, emotions are stored in different areas of the body. It is for this reason why it is important to nurture and take care of your body. Since this body is where we live, by taking care of it, it takes care of us. Then, we can go to the next step of releasing the stored emotions.

Next, we have a brain (our mind) which stores our different levels of consciousness for thinking, recording information (learning), sorting things out and making decisions.

One level of consciousness is called our subconscious mind, which records our thoughts, emotions, experiences and information that is given to us. This is a sort of library that we have in the subconscious mind that brings to the conscious mind what information we need. For example, just when you think you cannot remember someone's name, and then suddenly you remember it. That information was pulled from the subconscious mind. This is also where we store the memory of experiences, emotions and fears. Actually, all the seeds that have been planted whether positive or negative are in the memory banks of our subconscious mind. The memory of certain emotions come forth into our conscious mind whether we are looking for them or not. It usually happens when a condition that we are experiencing triggers a past thought, be it positive or negative which will make us feel that emotion or fear again. The subconscious mind is the library where we store all of our thoughts and feelings. Through these, we create our reality…our world.

The next level of consciousness is the conscious mind. The conscious mind is what we operate and think through during our waking hours. It puts us in the present time and is where we are. We use our conscious mind to act through and edit our thoughts and feelings. The conscious mind gives us the ability to evaluate conditions and to choose from them. The conscious mind is where choices are made. It makes the decision to react and act upon the situations which are presented before us each moment. It looks at our past experiences by our subconscious reminding us with positive or negative views, and it also looks ahead for our future experiences.

We also have what is called the supraconscious or superconscious mind where we can tap into the Divine source. This is our highest level of consciousness that we have within us. This is where we connect to the spark of God Intelligence or Divine consciousness. It is the part of us that is all knowing and is within us. This connection is opened by focusing on it through your conscious mind. This is where we get inspiration and where creative work is done.

So in all, we have these levels of consciousness to live through and create our world.

- The subconscious mind: our library of experiences and emotions. The *past mind*.

- The conscious mind: where we are and what we live through each day. The *present mind.*
- The supraconscious mind: our higher connection to Divine source and creation. The *future mind.*

Next, we have our heart in which we feel with. There is a lot of struggle sometimes with the brain trying to be logical and the heart going on what *feels* right. Once we can open the heart enough with unconditional love, we can start thinking more through the heart and usually get more accurate answers for better decisions. A lot of work needs to be done in expanding the heart area. This is where a lot of us are closed down due to fears or past pain. Still the mind and put your focus in your heart area, be open to the love already in your heart, expand it and be open to let love enter in. This is where the connection lies. The heart is the doorway to the supraconscious mind.

We also have the part of us that we have to live with that tries to rule our thoughts and emotions. It is the ego. The ego is our ying-yang so to speak. It has a negative charge and a positive charge. It is the human challenge that we carry. The challenge is to keep it in balance. The ego, the part of our mortal self, is in our subconscious mind and we all know how easily it is brought forth into the conscious mind. Whether you have low self-esteem or high self-esteem it does not seem to matter, the ego is still there. The negative side of ego seems to put us into a duality mode, a feeling of separateness that feeds on negative emotions. The positive side of ego maintains our respectability and how we present ourselves to the world. What we need is to keep the ego in proper balance.

So, we have a great challenge. The challenge of keeping all of the elements in balance by being in a physical body, in a physical world, which carries the positive and negative traits of ego, emotions of all levels, and different levels of consciousness. We also have the spark of God within us...our connection to life. We have a complete vehicle, equipped with everything we need, all of which we have a choice of how to operate. What thoughts, words or actions do we want to live through? This is the key.

Fear Not—Want Not

▼

PSALM 34:4
I sought the Lord, and he heard me, and
Delivered me from all my fears

We all seem to have fears and there are fears for every-thing. Not only phobias, like fear of flying, fear of spiders, fear of the dark, etc. but fear of things like not being suc-cessful, fear of being successful, fear of not finding the right mate, fear when finding the right mate, fear of not having enough money, fear of having everything. Can you believe that we can have a fear of attaining what we have a fear of never having. I know it does not seem to make sense. However, if you think about some of the fears you have had in the past, I am sure you can come up with some of these similarities. Through these fears, we create what we have and what we have lack of.

Here is an exercise. One day, take account of every time you felt afraid of something-when you had thoughts such as "I am afraid I'll miss my appointment", or "I am afraid that I will not have enough." Once you are conscious of your fears, you will become quite surprised by how many you have. In actuality, all of our needs are met and there is no need for fear or worry.

Remember back when you were young and went to Sunday School. You were taught about God and faith. As adults, still remembering some of the early Golden Rules, we go to church or continue some sort of spiritual practice that shows clearly that there is no need for fear or worrying about being without.

MATTHEW 6:30-34

30 *Wherefore, if God so clothe the grass of the field, which today is, and to-morrow is cast into the oven, shall he not much more clothe you, O ye of little faith?*

31 *Therefore take no thought, saying, What shall we eat? Or, What shall we drink? Or, Wherewithal shall we be clothed?*

32 *For your heavenly Father knoweth that ye have needed of all these things.*

33 *But seek ye first the kingdom of God, and his right-eousness, and all these things shall be added unto you.*

34 *Take therefore no thought for the morrow, for the morrow shall take thought for the things of itself, Sufficient unto the day is the evil thereof.*

This is one of the most common fears…the fear that we will not have what we need.

When you can release these fears, worries and anxieties you have and hold faith and trust in God, with the belief that all your needs *will* be met (and I mean *truly* believe), guest what-it happens! I am not saying this is easy to do. After all, we are used to the fear pattern. We have been using it all our lives. Just be conscious of each fear that arises and work with letting it go. You no longer need it, you are stronger than the fear. Fear is just a thought floating through you conscious mind. It is up to you how you let the fear affect you. If you let the fear affect you, then you will continue to be in need. God can only give you what you allow Him to. Know that all your needs are met, by just completely trusting in Him. As long as what you need is a *real* need and will cause no harm, it can be given to you. Through your conscious direction, you will have things or you will not have the things you need. Your fear keeps your needs from you. Only when letting go of the fear and allowing your needs to be fulfilled, will they manifest.

When you look back to circumstances that have left you without and then look at where you are today, can you see that everything comes to you in the right timing? I know that for myself, when one door closes, that means that a better door is ready to open. By understanding this, you will have something to look forward to, when a door closes for you. Do not feel dismayed about your situation. If you seem to be in an unhappy position and you do not understand why you are there and are miserable, just *know* that you are there for a reason. We may not ever know the *reason* why, but by continuing on without doubt, fear, or worry, then your new door will open to send you to your next step which is better.

One time in my life, I had left a job of many years, in order to start my own business. It did not work out. I ended up taking a job that made me miserable, but I held on because I needed the job. I would come home with knots in my stomach and crying because I was so miserable there. Each day, I prayed, please God, show me the lesson I need to learn and get me out of there. Within a few weeks, things fell into place and I got a job that was much better than any one that I had ever had. So, looking back I can see that if I had never taken the step to try starting my own business, even though it did not work out, it got me to the job where I have been the most successful and the happiest.

So, do not let your thinking be filled with fear and doubt, this is the power *you* give it. Where your focus and thought is, is where *you* are. Where your focus goes, your energy flows. Why not instead have confidence in God. This is an example of the subconscious mind sending thoughts to your conscious mind, but it is up to you to keep it as fear or filter it out. This is conscious mind choosing. It is your choice and decision that will result in the outcome of any situation.

You can choose happiness and joy trusting that all your needs are met. Or you can choose to live in fear where you get stuck and nothing happens resulting in unhappiness.

By choosing happiness, you will be saving yourself a lot of pain and wasted energy and we have to remember, these emotions are not healthy for the body. I remember my mother telling me when I was young that the mind controls the body. The mind also controls your world. It took me years to fully understand that statement, and how true it is. As what you are thinking, is so what you are doing. What thoughts you have will make your body react and act upon. Trust in God and *let* Him, *allow* Him to open the door for you.

This has happened throughout my life and I can see all the steps along the way that have brought me where I am today. The more you fill your conscious mind with believing and trusting God, and the more you do so without doubt, the faster the higher doors open for you. This will also help to cancel out negative thoughts and memories that your subconscious mind brings forth. Think about this, and look over your life and see where you have been brought to. Now even if it seemed uncomfortable, it still brings you through better doors as long as you see everything in a positive light and *know* things are just the way they are supposed to be. Like a tapestry or blueprint. This is the life you have planned for yourself. This is how far you have come.

It is also very important to let go of the past and only look ahead. Today is in the present and that is where we want to be. Let's not waste today on the yesterdays that are no more. We have so many beautiful tomorrows to look forward to.

As you will see later, that where you are today is exactly where you have *let* yourself be. This is as far as you have *allowed* yourself to go. Fear is a strong emotion and will take some work to dissolve. When you have even the slightest sense of fear of not obtaining something for instance, the fear holds it back. The fear is in your thoughts and feelings.

The same goes for having fears that something may happen. Thoughts are creations. For example, when I was young and walked to school when the streets were icy, I was always afraid that I would fall, and yes, I fell quite often.

Thoughts are important. Listen to your every thought and you will be surprised at how many of those thoughts are worries and concerns. All of these thoughts can be turned around to positive ones and be let go of. Fears are lodged in your subconscious mind which is your past mind. The past is over and done with…get over it. It does not have to be part of your world anymore. Where do you want to be? Living and re-living the past or creating a beautiful today and tomorrow?

Like anything in life, nothing can exist if it is not fed. When you have any negative thoughts or words of fear, you are feeding your fears and keeping them stronger than ever. In actuality, your fears need you to keep feeding them with worry or they would not be able to exist.

Once you have decided not to feed these fears, they will die away from lack of *food*. If we were able to see from a higher level how we let the fears and emotions control our body and world, it would be shocking.

Have you ever looked back at something you had a fear about long ago and realized that since you have let that fear go, whatever you were afraid of then, does not bother you now? When a fear comes up, stop and look at it as though it is something separate from you. This is an important step, to make it not a part of you anymore.

You may find out the reality of the origin of the fear, or you may not right away. Just look at it and know that you no longer need it and you will no longer allow it to bother you. Tell the fear that "I do not give you further power to act in my world." "You have no power to affect, limit, or disturb me again." This is a way of re-programming your subconscious mind by showing it that this is no longer allowed. Once you get used to standing up to these fears and dissolving them, you will feel stronger. Soon, it will be as easy as pulling a plug to get rid of the fears. Do not feed your fears anymore!

As you go through these steps:
Let go of the fear and step through the doorway.
Take the passage into the rest of your life.

Open Your Eyes

Many things in life will catch your eye,
But only a few will catch your heart
Persue those...
Author unknown

It is hard to imagine that some people can go their entire lives and barely notice the beauty this world has to offer. Of course, we have human beauty. Whether it be a beautiful child or a beautiful adult. As for the child, we see them as perfect and innocent. Something that we used to have or be. As for the beautiful adult, we see them for their physical beauty, which most people are attracted to.

Just look at all the magazines with models and in the movies at all the actresses and actors that are supposed to signify a "model" for beauty. In a world such as now, it is hard to keep up our looks and that youthful beauty we had when we were in our 20's. When we see someone with physical beauty, we admire them so, because it is hard to attain or maintain. We like to be around them because it seems that they know something we do not, or that they have attained something that we all can have. We all want to recapture our beauty. That beauty that we know deep inside that we are. We admire someone who may have the secret.

But now let us talk about *true beauty.* Have you ever looked into someone's eyes and seen that spark of light? That connection to their soul. As we have all heard, the eyes are the windows to the soul. How true that is. Please try this if you have not experienced this. No need to put up walls, we are all connected. Just look *deep* into their eyes and feel that connection to their soul. You can even see a bit of their truth. It can bring tears to your eyes. Try to see that divine spark in everyone. True beauty is within each of us. Identify with this beauty and beam this out to the world and be this true beauty.

With beauty, we recognize and are attracted to the external forms of it because we are not yet ready to accept our internal *embodiment* of beauty. Once we realize that we embody the God essence that is already within us, we will cease grasping for the tangible perfection that we think we see. We keep trying to perfect our external appearances when, if we achieved beauty and grace in our inner selves, we would reflect this in our outer selves to the world. This is one of the best examples of the world of opposites…the paradox. The challenge of the body we walk the earth with.

Not to say there is anything wrong with cosmetic surgery. I think it is great! If there is something that you are not happy with, then fix it. People can really obsess about a so called physical imperfection and focus on it to the point that it keeps them from being happy. If this is the case then just go fix it! The sooner you are satisfied with your external appearance, then you can focus on your inner self, your inner true beauty.

After all, physical beauty is splendid to behold, but its significance is only fleeting if it is not accompanied by the most important inner beauty. For all of the physically beautiful people out there, remember, you are not truly beautiful until you have let go of your ego about being physically beautiful. Then, you need to work on your inner beauty to let the *true beauty* radiate from every cell of your being. This goes for everyone who has not seen this in others, or who has not done their inner beauty work. It does not matter if you are old, young, short, tall, fat, thin, physically pretty or not. See it in everyone. Look into their eyes and see it.

The truth of the matter is, as we let go of our emptiness inside (the emptiness is the only place false beliefs can hide) and realize that what we embody is God essence. Then work on expanding God's essence from the inside out, then only beauty can there be. Work with yourself and feel the God essence inner beauty that you are. Know this and accept it. Let it flow through you and send it out to everyone, everyday. It will just bubble forth from your heart. People will see it in your eyes. Thus, the true key to eternal youth. For as you resonate to your true inner beauty and *be* that beauty, it radiates out into your physical form. You will have an incredible glow about you.

> *Only certain things from outer expression*
> *Can feed the inner spirit*

God has given us a beautiful world in which to live. Go out in nature more often. Look at the beautiful plants, flowers, trees, waterfalls, lakes, oceans, mountains, sunsets and sunrises. Listen to the birds singing and the touch of a breeze against your skin. See everything as through the eyes of a child. See the wonder of everything God has created. Experience the animals, the children, the different cultures. There is a whole world to see and experience. See life as the miracle that it is and you will see beauty that you never dreamed of. Just open your eyes.

> On this day, for every eyes mine meet
> May I send God's love for them
> To *see* and *be*.

Be Kind And Harmless

▼

If there is any kindness I can show, or any good thing
I can do for any fellow being, let me do it now, and not defer it
Or neglect it, as I shall not pass this way again.
                                        -William Penn

If it is our true nature to want people to be kind and harmless to us, why are some people so unkind and harmful? Though it goes back to their earlier programming, anyone can change their attitude and manner of being by being conscious of their actions.

We have to start with our thoughts, words, and actions. These are the creating forces in our world. It only takes a few moments of irritation or criticism to hold ourselves back and depriving ourself of happiness. By acting in this manner, we are choosing limitation.

Start thinking in a kind way about everything in your world, choosing the right words that are not offensive and will not hurt anyone. Watch your emotions and reactions to things. I guess we could all try to think twice before we speak, especially when reacting to a situation. Keep from criticizing each other. Have instead only feelings of kindliness and blessing.

Resentment usually precipitates anger. Anger is a very destructive emotion. It is like a barking dog that is hard to control. I know it can be hard when you are feeling angry but try to clear this emotion and let it go. You would not want someone you love to be in anger, and the same goes for you. Harsh negative emotions deteriorate the body. As mentioned earlier, what stress can do to the body. Remember, that the more harsh the emotion, the more harsh you are on your body. When you have feelings of anger, fear, jealousy, hatred…you know…the harsh emotions. It is a burning feeling isn't it? It is literally burning you up and eating away at you inside, therefore, the major cause of physical disease, poor health and deterioration of the body.

Let us understand that all unhappiness is of our own creation. Whatever we are allowing to cause disturbance or irritation in our feelings is of our own creation holding us to the bonds of limitation. This self-limitation is of our own doing. Only we can limit ourselves, no one else can.

Try to keep watch of your feelings and not allow any disturbance to take over. The more you can stop the negative feeling right away, the sooner the negativity will leave you alone. Each time it tries to enter, pull its plug. It will have no more power. Once you do not allow disturbing

thoughts to enter your mind, this will result in more feelings of happiness flowing through your consciousness. You
will live life much more joyfully.

People can never be happy if they are self-absorbed and
never care about others. This behavior is a result of their
earlier negative programming, and their way of protecting
themselves. This need not be so. True happiness needs to
come from within.

Once you are willing to change your attitude to kindness and stop yourself when you are acting self-absorbed
(of course, first becoming aware of your behavior and
being able to admit it to yourself) then you will automatically be reprogramming yourself...your subconscious way
of acting. Our actions should always be a result of good
intentions to others.

You have the power over your thoughts and feelings.
Try not to get involved in other peoples drama. If that is
where they want to be, let them, you do not need to go
there. By using self-control over your feelings, you will
never have the desire again to feel irritated, disturbed or
have a single opinion about anyone except to send them
love and blessings and to wish them well. This change of
attitude will make you feel much better inside and is
therefore healing to your self and your spirit. Anyway, is it
not much nicer to send a blessing rather than a bad
thought?

Try this for a day and then for a week. I assure you that
you will see a big difference in how you feel about daily

situations and people. You will find that each day is not so hard and you will be genuinely happy for the new day and others will notice the difference in you.

This has to be *real* acts of kindness and harmlessness truly meant from your heart or it will not work. Do something for someone that you have never done before. Encourage someone by compliment or by pointing out the positive qualities you see in them. Be verbal, sometimes the slightest kind word could change someone's life for the better. This course of action will definitely change your life for the better.

"My true religion is kindness."
-The Dali Lama

After a while you will enjoy this renewed positive energy flowing through you, and you will shine from every pore. People will respond to this way of being treated. It is the way we all want to be treated. As you pour forth love and kindness to everyone, then your world will be flooded with all good things.

If, in every relation you have with someone, you treat them with the utmost respect, the purest intention and kindness, and they treat you in return in the same manner, then I cannot see how there can be so many problems. This alone could save many marriages. Your relationship would have a sacred sense and from the heart, therefore promoting a healthy bond. By making this your way of being, your whole life will change for the better.

SHAME ON US

▼

PSALMS 4:2

O ye sons of men, how long
Will ye turn my glory into shame?

We are all here on planet Earth. We are not Americans, Australians or Africans so much as we are all, what I like to call, Earthians. We are here to live the human experience, and through this, work our way back to God.

Jesus came to show us the way, but truly, only a few take note. Yes, a lot of us go to different kinds of churches and have different faiths in search of the way-the truth, the path-but sadly, only a few truly *live* the works and words they are taught. Words without the works behind them mean nothing in the kingdom of God.

Every moment we are given opportunities to live, move and have our being (think, speak, and act) in a Christ-like manner, which includes unconditional love, thinking of others before yourself, do no-thing to hurt another (includes gossiping), trust in God, if not, then you will continue to have the same lessons confronting you. If you keep treating others unkindly, you will see the same situations presented to you until you make the positive choice. Kindness is much better than being mean. Think of treating others the way you want others to treat you.

How do you think we are doing as humans on the lesson of loving one another unconditionally, and holding no judgment, criticism or hatred of others? Just from what I see, I think we are doing poorly. I wonder what it looks like from Heaven. This is real proof of a patient God. How can we be so impatient?

Now is a good time to start over with thoughts of unconditional love and kindness to one another and to ourselves. We must not forget to be kind and love ourselves as well. Send this all over the world. Not just in your little group or community. Just think what a change could take place on the planet if everyone would simply be kind and not hurt one another.

When you are acting in an unkind negative way, you are only hurting yourself by holding your own spiritual progress back. Remember that through your deeds you are either progressing or holding yourself back. Keep guard of your thoughts, feelings, and words. It takes conscious awareness and daily practice. If you think that just because you are a good person is enough, then you are mistaken. There is much more to it than that. There are a lot of good people out there that still let negative situations come into their thoughts and feelings which end up taking over their world. For a start, try to think, speak and act in a loving manner in everything you do. Start seeing the good in everyone and everything.

There is a Christian logo that I absolutely LOVE! It is WWJD. It stands for WHAT WOULD JESUS DO? If that does not say it all, I do not know what does. Just observe your thoughts and actions and see if you are acting in a Christ-like manner. Are you handling each situation in a kind and loving manner? How would you want someone to respond to you given the same situation? If you need an answer about a problem, just ask yourself, what would Jesus do in this situation? Your answer will come to you quite obviously without doubt. You know the heart that Jesus has and you know what is the right thing to do.

There Is No Better Than...Only Different

▼

Earth is the institution for the spiritually confused
In hopes of enlightenment.

We are all connected. We come from the same place (from God) and we are going back to the same place (back to God). So why is there all this separation and duality? We feel separate from God and make it worse by making ourselves separate from each other. Separate nations, separate governments, laws, religions, races, businesses, relationships and on and on. Anything that causes a rivalry between one another is separate from God. There is NO BETTER THAN...ONLY DIFFERENT.

Being different means variety. That is what makes this earth so enjoyable. Different flowers, trees, species of animals, foods, climates, seasons, terrain,....humans. So why not enjoy all the varieties and not be negative, criticize, or hate others because of their differences. Life is about experiencing and having the pleasures of life's variety. Do you think a rose dislikes the tulip because it is different or that the oak would have a war with the pines because they are different? I think not. God created us all to be equal. God placed us on the same planet for some reason. I am sure it was not to watch us have rivalries and end up killing one another because we look different or speak differently. It was for the variety! Would you want to wear the same outfit every day or eat only one type of food every day? Of course not. This proves our human need for variety. We should have respect for one another because we come from the same place. No one is better than anyone else, they are only different from one another. Let us try to make an effort to learn more about differences and variety around the world and respect them.

I think it would be great if children could experience all the different cultures, countries and religious beliefs around the world as they grow up as part of their schooling. These kinds of experiences would surely contribute to the individual being more compassionate and tolerant as an adult.

I grew up in the South where there was a lot of segregation. Even in my young child's heart I felt that this was not right. It did not seem right, to keep people separated because of their color. I was probably only about eight years old when one day, a little girl was being ushered to the back of the bus because of the color of her skin. I caught her eyes and kept them there trying to let her know

I didn't agree with all this. I think she understood me because she finally gave me a smile.

It does not matter what you have been taught as a child as to the way things are. Think with your heart and know what is right. Raise yourself above the human conception. The human idea of what is good, bad, right or wrong is not always the truth as far as God is concerned. Look deep and hard at the human ideas and see what you feel.

As an illustration, imagine somebody who considers himself wealthy, with all forms of material success, comes across someone walking down the street and they look homeless or destitute. Is it not the first sense of the wealthy one to look down upon the homeless one and feel better than they are? Unfortunately, it is so, and that my friends, is the ego speaking, for no matter what your financial status is, for no matter what you have, you are **no** better that the homeless one on the street. This is where the ego comes in. We need to recognize this and not let the negative ego be in control each time it shows itself. It can be very tricky. Because of our earlier programming, the subconscious mind will bring the ego into play at any opportunity. Each time you stop yourself from letting your ego get the better of you, then you are re-programming your subconscious mind. This helps to balance the ego. Most of our conscious mind hours are spent in negative ego, and we have spent years there. It will take daily conscious effort to balance this into the positive side of ego and consciousness. Exercises to help with this process are given in the following chapters.

God is not so much interested in your material gain. What He is interested in is your humbleness, kindness and love toward each other. True riches have **nothing** to do with material possessions. True riches come from unconditional love and living the life of God-connected-consciousness. In other words, having the Divine God connected way of thinking and doing…in your consciousness. This is already a part of us, in our supraconscious mind. It is not up to us to judge one another for what point they are at in their existence. Have no concern of anything else except the cleansing and clearing of your own mind, body and world. Be not concerned about someone else when it comes to what stage that each of you are in the world.

Remember, where you are right now is where you have allowed yourself to be. Do not judge another for where he or she is. Just smile and send them a blessing, and have humility. You will honestly feel much better by sending a blessing rather than a bad thought.

There is nothing wrong with having material success as long as you have acquired it honestly and from a humble nature and not using it for feeding your ego. Just as on the other hand, there is nothing wrong with having less and living a more simple life but, not to judge others or have envy for ones who have more material possessions than you do. Be happy with who you are and content with what you have.

There are also some of us who feel they are superior because of the education that they have had. Education and knowledge are two completely different things. Just because you may have had many years of college and hold impressive degrees does not mean you have *any* knowledge of life in general or your spiritual nature. This is what really matters. Spiritual knowledge is the highest level of *education* to be attained while we are here. This is *why* we are here. To work our way through the physical body to get back to God. God made each one of us equal in His eyes. It is only our own negative human ideas that set us apart. Let us not have the better than thou attitude. I have seen this attitude mainly in three categories: of people who feel wealthy, with ones who feel highly educated, and with ones who feel physically beautiful. All three categories convey a sense of superiority to others. Interestingly, the three things that most everyone would want in their life can be their own worst enemy.

Balance the ego. When we can remember that and treat each other with the same respect as we wish to be treated, it will make a big difference in the world and in your world.

MATHEW 5; 44-45

44　*But I say unto you, Love your enemies, bless them that curse you, do good to them that hate you, and pray for them which despitefully use you, and persecute you;*

45　*That ye may be the children of your Father which is in heaven; for he maketh his sun to rise on the evil and on the good, and sendeth rain on the just and on the unjust.*

Remember, we are God's *variety* who have been given the privilege to inhabit planet Earth during our lifetime. This privilege does not include the right to fight, hate and kill one another because they are different than we are. All it takes is a commitment to change our thoughts, words, feelings, actions and attitudes toward each other.

We can all co-habitate on this planet, working together, and not against each other. Live your life with a sense of joy, love, kindness to one another, integrity, compassion and avoid separateness. Remember, you are holding yourself back with negative behavior. Do not blame others for your unhappiness or continue to blame your childhood for your negative behavior. It is up to you to work on cleansing and clearing the past through forgiveness and letting go. It is only you that can make your own progress by changing your attitude and letting go of the past. Get over it and get on with life. It is only you who keeps yourself behind and unhappy. It is up to *you*.

Forgive You-Forgive Me

▼

LUKE 23:34

Then said Jesus, Father, forgive them;
For they know not what they do.

Forgiving is another word for loving. Just as parents love
their children so very much, that they easily forgive them
for things that they do because their love is so great for
them. This is in a parallel sense, except at an even greater
level, how God forgives us for things we do and still loves
us very much. At least a parent has a chance to interact
with their child on a physical level, face to face. We can
talk things over and work our problems out.

Just imagine how many people go day to day, week to
week, year through years and do not give God (our true
Father) a thought or even acknowledge all that He has
given to us, by his continued love and forgiveness. If a
human parent were similarly not acknowledged for what

they have done for us, that parent would be quite upset and probably not have a very good relationship with that child because of our human need of acknowledgement for *what I have done for you.* This also is true with any relationship…friends, family, mates. We have all felt this way with someone in our life.

Fortunately, our Father in Heaven is patient and forgiving. True forgiveness is for-giving to others unconditionally. This means doing things and giving to others without expecting anything in return. The human sense is for us to have something in return for what we are giving, whether it be love, friendship or material things. True love means giving love unconditionally, even without expecting anything in return. This is probably one of the hardest lessons to try: to love someone even when you know that they will not or may not love you in return. This is what the word unconditional means: that you are not putting any conditions on giving or receiving love. What makes it hard is the part of our being human, filled with senses and emotions.

When we can transcend to the point of just giving love, being love, and having the expectation of only Gods love in return, this is a quantum leap in our spiritual development. We want to feel love, but feel separate from God and that is where our need for human love comes from. The truth of the matter is that we have always, and will always, have Gods love with us every moment of our lives. Acknowledge this fact and feel it. Let love be the governing principle in your world.

Weigh the true advantages of forgiveness
and resentment to the heart. Then choose.
                                    -The Buddha

If someone has done something to you that you feel that they owe you an apology, you can forgive them either by telling them or truly forgiving them in your heart. Most of the time, it is just our ego that has been hurt, so it is a good lesson for balancing the ego. Of course, there is a fine line between having a giving nature and being taken advantage of. You can be meek but powerful. You can be humble and strong all at the same time.

We have what is called our Divine destiny or Divine plan. The mission that we came here to accomplish. Life takes us through many doors, up and down many steps until we reach our destiny, our true plan that we are looking for.

Any relationship that did not work out was a gift and part of the Divine destiny that you have mapped out for yourself. Think of every relationship and friendship that came through your life. Each one was a step along the way. Look at each one in a state of neutrality. Forgive them if they hurt you and thank them for pushing you through the next door.

If you had not had this experience to spurn yourself on, you may have just *settled* for where you were and not gone onward and upward to where you were truly meant to be.

Now, try thinking of someone that has hurt you. Just to yourself, forgive them in your heart. If this is hard a first, try again each day. Soon you will find that you have really forgiven them and whatever the reason was for the hurt, it does not seem to matter any more. When you think of the situation and you still feel hurt, then you have not yet completely forgiven them. Try again. Forgiveness can bring you gratefulness to that person. They helped you take your next step. Not only forgive them, but thank them. Free yourself, your spirit, and your soul.

Then the next step would be of course, to think of someone that *you* have hurt and feel in your heart how great it would feel to contact them and let them know how you feel and truly ask for their forgiveness. If you cannot contact them, then ask for their forgiveness from your heart and let it go.

It is also important to forgive yourself for things that you have done. Once you can come to terms with and recognize what you have done that is not in alignment with God, ask for His forgiveness and know it has been released.

EP HESIANS 4:32

> *32: And be ye kind one to another, tenderhearted, forgiving one another, even as God for Christ's sake hath forgiven you.*

Forgiveness is one of the most healing things that you can do for yourself. As you truly forgive the ones who have hurt you, this is then released from your being and world, which in turn sets you free. It sets you free to allow into your life that which is from your Divine plan. We all have a Divine plan, a Divine destiny which can only come into play when we release the past pain and emotion attached to the past which when holding on to, holds us back. We will usually hold on to it until we are completely ready and accepting to proceed with our Divine plan.

In some ways, this serves a purpose...to hold on and when we let go, it is the right time and it lets go of us. Whatever we are holding on to is thereby holding on to us to serve as we consciously direct. Once we are willing to let go, the things we are holding on to sees that its purpose is served and starts to let go of us at the same time, when the timing is right. Consider too, that sometimes what we are holding on to, lets go first, therefore compelling us to let go which moves us onward to our higher purpose.

God has everything so perfectly set for us. It is just up to us to listen and surrender to the plan...our own plan we asked God to set for us. Surrender to the Divine plan and watch it unfold.

Let us learn to forgive one another and learn from our mistakes of hurting someone. Treat others as you would want to be treated. Do onto others *truly* as you would have them do onto you. Would you really want someone to think negatively, lie, gossip, steal, or treat you unfairly? Then why would you ever dream of doing this to someone else?

There is the Universal Law of energy. If you put these negative intentions out it will come back to you. Life is all about energy, and all energy is sent back to its original source. Your negative intentions may not return to you from the same person you sent it to, but by someone else.

All it takes is a change in attitude toward others and you can be the first to start. After a while, people will see you for the example that you have set and will want to do the same. Once you understand how to use this universal law of energy, it can be a very powerful tool to change your life for the better.

Every day we are set before trials and lessons to learn from. Look at each one as an opportunity to use these laws and better your life. Be aware before you take any action with every relationship that you have, and see if you can handle yourself in a positive, giving and loving way.

This IS our true nature, to treat others and be treated in a kind and harmonious manner. The great challenge is by being in our physical bodies and to work through the emotions and fears that we carry. Do not let another day go by without remembering what we are meant to do...what our true essence is. For-giving to others.

Turn Your World Around

"It is within you that the Divine lives."
                              -Joseph Campbell

So far, we have taken a look at ourselves and can see where the roots of our personal problems lie. It is important to remember that it can all be turned around.

Have you ever been driving when you have come onto a roundabout where you must choose which road you are going to take or else you will just keep going in circles? Which leads you back to the same place over and over and not getting anywhere. Does this sound like your life? Do you feel stuck and just going in circles? The first thing to do is to take the step with intention and purpose to get onto the right road and get off the roundabout. I know it can be scary at first and you may think you will not survive. Things are moving so much faster than you are used to. You must take your step with intention and purpose to get onto the right path and keep driving without any fear or worry. If any fear crops up, just let it go. Do not let it affect you. Know that everything is in its right place.

Everything happens exactly how it is supposed to. Just take a moment to look around you. Listen, look, smell, feel. Everything is exactly how it is supposed to be for you have *put* yourself there. If you find you are not happy with where you are, then it is up to you my friend, to make a change. For where you are in this moment is not bad…it is only as far as you have *allowed* yourself to come. Everything is waiting for you. It is at your door. Sometimes you say you are ready, but you still have that little fear, that doubt that will not allow what you want into your world.

How many times have you dreamed about achieving something, only to give up out of fear when it seems like you just might reach your goal or worst of all, think that you are not worthy? I know from experience about this one.

Matthew 6:33

But seek ye first the kingdom of God, and his righteousness; and all these things shall be added unto you.

You *can* attain any goal you desire and you *are* worthy to have a wonderful life. This is not just for the chosen few. As long as your intention is good and you are not wishing for things out of greed or for feeding your ego. As long as your heart is pure and you are living a truly loving life without fear and doubt, then all your needs will be met. There is no limit to Gods treasure chest, there is enough for everyone. You will always be provided for of everything that you need. Maybe not everything you want…if it is not really needed. Do you really *need* to have a million dollars? Do you really *need* a new car every year? Do you really *need* closets full of clothes and shoes that mostly are never worn (I know this one well). It seems we women love to have pairs and pairs of shoes. I have spoken to many about this, almost like taking a survey and I know this is true for a lot of women. It seems to relate to wanting to step into a new direction.

Eventually, it is time to do a closet clearing of sorts. Does it not feel good to clear out cabinets and closets of things that you do not really need and give it away? As we start doing this in a physical sense, will start our inner clearing. Let go of things that no longer serve you. Everything goes full circle; you will not have the things that you properly need in your life if you do not release the old stuff. Inside and out. As you start to let go of external material things that you no longer need, you can start focusing on letting go of internal old thought patterns and feelings too. There is a lot of cleaning and clearing to do in every area of our life.

Everything is a constant flow of energy. Everything in life at every moment is moving. Just like the wind and the ocean is constantly moving. Nothing in nature stays stagnate. Life is about constant flow…the river of Life.

Let's take a look at money. The currency in the United States is imprinted with "In God We Trust." I think that is a good clue to trust in God and not have any negative concerns about money. We use this money every day, not even taking note what words are printed on it. Money is NOT a bad thing. Only when you view money as bad or think that money is the root of evil. It is not.

You probably will also know people that, on the other hand, have a lot of money and are stingy in spending it. That is because they are afraid they will lose it and in fear of not get more back. These people will let money rule their life and world. Of course they will get more in return when using it for the right purposes and not being in fear of losing it. It has to come back to you. It is the Universal Law of energy.

It is important to understand that anything you put out you will receive the same back. Love begets love, joy begets joy, positive begets positive. Remember however, that this also applies for negative begets negative, dislike begets dislike, fear begets fear, which will result in unhappiness begets more unhappiness. It is up to you to stay with the circle of unhappiness, continually going around and coming back to where you were before. It is time to get off the roundabout and get onto your right path and keep driving!

LETTING GO

"Freedom Comes from letting the
Higher Force Guide Your Life"
B.G.

Letting go has everything to do with surrender. Letting go of fear is a good start. Letting go of all false beliefs that have held you back and kept you going in circles. Like the belief that things always go wrong, that is only your disbelief, especially if things are going right, you think, "Oh, that won't last." The truth is the opposite of this disbelief and actually, things can *always go right* for the rest of your life, depending on your belief or disbelief. All these disbeliefs are fear based. Such as, "I doubt this or that will happen "or "I fear about this or that." When we can get started on positive living, we can cut the cords of disbelief.

When you have total faith and trust in God that everything is going to be all right then it *will*. We just need to watch our thoughts that they do not stray over to negative territory. We complicate matters much more than any-where near necessary. Letting go of fear and negativity with trusting in God is the first step. Next, we need to work on letting go of these emotions that are lodged in our subconscious mind and in our bodies. This has to do with cleansing and clearing the mind and the body. This takes daily conscious effort. Our future is set up by our conscious direction. Are you going to direct your con-sciousness in fear and worry, or let go of these emotions that do us no good. Which sounds better to you?

Now, let us look at our state of mind. For many people, when they go to church, it leaves them with that good feeling inside. They remember the sermon, the mass, the message for the rest of that day and are aware of their thoughts. By Monday, bits and pieces of the 'food for thought' sermon come in and out of their daily thoughts. By Tuesday, and for sure, by Wednesday, we are back to our old thought patterns and disbeliefs.

Why not keep the church going within the heart and consciousness all the time? Not just on Sunday, but every moment of the day, you can be in communion with God all the time. Keep your Sunday sermons going in every thought, word and action that you do. Be conscious of what you are thinking, feeling, saying and doing. After a while, it will be so automatic that if you were to even think a negative thought, you would be so consciously bothered about it, you would surprise yourself. With continual con-scious work like this, you will be in a constant state of hap-piness and bliss.

An easy way to start is to pray, meditate, or however you commune with God. Do this from the heart. Let Him know that you totally surrender to Him, that you totally trust Him. Qualify your prayers with glory to God, for it is all to the glory of Him. Lead your life in a manner that is only love, joy, generosity, honor, compassion and integrity. Once you make this commitment, and God knows your heart, you will feel a shift in your consciousness and being. Truly live by this commitment and just watch the doors open for you. Now, bear in mind that no matter where you are or whatever your conditions seem to be, this is always a step to the next door. Ask to be shown whatever lesson you need to learn and then you can move on. You will only move as fast as you *allow* yourself.

Picture yourself inside a huge plastic sphere (your world). On the outside are all these puzzle pieces that are your prayers and things that you have asked for and needed. All your prayers are heard. They are out there trying to fit into your world but *cannot* until you *allow* them in. Keep on with the absolute knowing that you will have these things in your life. Whatever, they are as long as it is for your highest good, cannot get in until you turn your disbeliefs around to true beliefs. Have complete faith. Trust in Gods plan and allow your puzzle pieces of life to come in. It does take, not only your faith but co-operation with God to achieve this.

When things have not happened the way you would have liked in life, and you feel that your faith in God is strong, then take a deeper look to see what fears are behind this holding it back. Then take another look at this and discern as to whether it is something you really need. Your ego can allow you to feel that you need something to where you want it really bad, even come up with very positive reasons for needing it. Just ask yourself, the truth, is this for me or for my ego? Do not let your ego control these situations.

Things also need to come in appropriate timing. I know at times when I wanted a certain situation in my life, I would tell God "I know that I am ready, please, oh pleeeese." But when I look at what changes I made in myself from the point of wanting this situation to the time when it happened, I can see what is meant by Divine timing and patience. If what I wanted had happened too soon, I would not have been ready (or as ready is I thought I was), and the outcome would not have been perfect. Patience is indeed a virtue.

If, this life experience is our learning station, our institution, then every experience we choose is a choice to learn from and step further ahead. If a situation did not work out, just know, it was the one you chose to go through the learning lesson with to get you to where you are supposed to be. It is just another step.

So, when you feel you have made a mistake, it really is not. A mistake is just a take of choice. It is what you needed to keep yourself on track to get yourself where you want to go.

So, when you have chosen to go into an experience, that seems so right, the perfect thing to do, but in the end, did not work out the way you thought it would. This is alright. Have no regrets. The outcome has brought you to a better step. We can only take these next steps when we are ready to move closer to our goal. Sometimes we feel we cannot trust our own judgment because the outcome was not what we thought it was going to be, and we do not want to make the same seeming mistake. Sometimes confirmation from a close friend helps with some of your decisions, but final decisions come from trusting your heart. Listen to your heart. You know where you need to be.

When you are working hard for something that you really want or trying to keep something that is yours and it does not work out, just know that how it turned out was how it was meant to be. Look at the situation and trust the knowing that God has a better plan and let go. Do not keep holding on. Try not to control others that may have different paths of life. When you can let go of things and let nature (God) take its course, you will see later *that* was how it was meant to be all the time and what better doors have opened.

What I have found in my life is that when you try to make things happen, is when you end up with a mess. Do not worry about what you may have lost, or who has left your life, because there is something or someone much better waiting for you.

"We must be willing to get rid of the life we've planned,
so as to have the life that is waiting for us."
                              -Joseph Campbell

By letting go of disbeliefs such as, the disbelief that you are the victim, or that you never have what you want in life. This is a disbelief. Turn this around and know that you will have the things in your life that you truly need and expect the miracle. Expect and allow the door to open and it will with complete faith. Do not accept anything less than perfection and expect nothing less. Re-affirm this every day. Affirmations are a great way to keep yourself focused on the positive. Some of my favorites are:

- With God all things are possible.
- There is only God in action here.
- I allow Divine love in my life.
- I allow God's plan.
- The light of God never fails.

God's will is good will...the birthright to everyone. Having free will, we must understand that God can only act in our life and world according to *our* conscious direction. This has everything to do with surrendering to God's will and not your will. Let go of all of *your* expectations, misconceptions and thoughts of how you think things are *supposed to be.* Forget it all. Start every day with a clean slate and allow God to orchestrate your world.

When you use your imagination or fantasize about how you want a situation to be, how you dream about things or how you want someone to respond to you...this is *your* will. This is why your dreams have not come true. You cannot say that you surrender to God's will and still have your own desires of how you want things.

Do not feel bad if your dream does not happen. God is saving you from a possible setback and you could be missing the opportunity that was meant for you. Of course, in planning your course of action for daily living, try and not use all your energy on your own desires. Leave it to God's will and let Him set things up for you.

Once we understand that it is us creating our own destiny, and then co-operate with God's will, then the Divine plan will fall into place. It makes life so much easier to give it all up to God and your life will unfold to your true destiny. Give everything up to God. He wants to ease the burden that we have put upon ourselves. As you give to God, you are actually giving to yourself.

Eventually, with this way of thinking and feeling, it leaves no room for worry about tomorrow. When you totally leave it all up to God's will, there is the truest sense of inner freedom. Just wait to see what tomorrow brings, without any thoughts attached to it. It makes every day like Christmas Eve, expecting only gifts and celebration. The only thing you have to look forward to, is waiting to see what God has planned for you. What freedom you can experience in your life!

I set my free will free…
So it may go see God
And bring only God back to me
I set my free will free…
So now I can only be of Gods will
To truly set me free…
I set my free will free

It is important to understand that thoughts are creations, that sets things into motion. It also sets up an emotion. For instance, when you make up a scenario in your mind, even though it has never happened, just the thought of experiencing the scene you have made up in your mind, can upset you when you imagine a negative outcome. You could also be limiting a better outcome that God has planned for you when you make up scenes of how you want things to happen…through projecting your will. Remember that all of these thoughts are being recorded into your subconscious library.

It is really quite funny, how we can get ourselves all worked up over a thought of something that has never happened. This self-inflicted pain should make us want to stop and think positive all the time.

During our conscious hours our mind is visualizing something continuously, every day. Just start trying to keep all else out of the mind except the picture you want for your highest good. Try not to let your attention become focused on emptiness. When a negative picture comes in, pluck it out right away. Focus on God's will and just have the knowing that the outcome of any situation that God has planned for you is better than anything you could have dreamed about.

Remember, you want God's will to be done not your own. It takes some practice in catching yourself as we daydream. I know because I catch myself all the time, but each time I realize what I am doing I stop myself and remind God that I truly want His will, not mine. I cannot

stress this point enough. It helps to keep reminding yourself to trust in God's plan. It will truly make a difference in
your life and it also frees up a lot of wasted energy.

The truth is, all you really need is to depend on God.
Honor Him with your thoughts, words and actions. Be
kind, patient, loving, giving, selfless, and have no need for
negativity or senseless desires. All your needs will be met
and much more as you surrender yourself to God. Let go
of all the old past thoughts, words and actions. Give them
up to God to take care of for you...then have no worry of
them again.

It is important to understand that you are controlling
your complete reality and destiny. Your thoughts and feelings are the creating powers in your world. Also consider
the creating power of the word. Not only do we create
through our thoughts and feelings, but our words. Be conscious of your conversations and suggestions. For what
you speak is brought forth.

If you seem bothered or disturbed about something,
the more you think about it, the more power it has over
you. This is like throwing gasoline to a flame.
Remember, that was then and this is now. The now is all
there is. Be in the present. Let go of all your past fears,
doubts, worries and negativity. Set your Divine plan
into action. Stop and listen to what you are thinking
and saying. Is this coming from the ego? You will know
the answer right away. If so, work on balancing the negative ego. Do not let it control you. You control it.
When your ego is balanced and you are in control, you

have more pure thoughts, pure intentions. Have no need for competition, or need to have more than what others have. All these petty mortal needs that we have can consume our entire life. Just think how free we can feel by not feeding into the negativity of ourselves. Once you let go, you have room to let your puzzle pieces fit into your world. Let go and Let God.

Broken Dreams

As children bring their broken toys
With tears for us to mend,
I brought my broken dreams to God
Because He was my friend,

But instead of leaving Him
In peace to work alone,
I hung around and tried to help,
With ways that were my own.

At last I snatched them back
And cried "how can you be so slow?"
"My child," He said, "what could I do?
You never did let go."

-author unknown

Seeing the Light

Let your light so shine before men,
that they may see your good works,
and glorify your Father which is in heaven
Matthew 5:16

Now that you have been able to start letting go, you will notice shifts taking place in your life. You will start looking at the world and everything in a totally different perspective. Everything will seem brighter, things that used to bother you just do not matter anymore. Your Divine plan is coming into action. You have stopped giving energy to negativity and slowly it leaves you alone. When you stop feeding these false ideas with what they want…fear and worry, then they simply cannot exist anymore, they just fall away.

As you can live your life more and more like this, then it leaves only room for God's light to come in. When you start looking at the world through the light coming in, everything starts to change not only in your world but in the world around you. By making this your way of being, people will see the light coming out through you. As everything goes full circle, and you project the light, the goodness out to the world, it comes back to you. Positive goes out, positive comes back. Good goes out, good comes back and you will start to notice that what you start getting back is more and more. The more you give out, the more you get back. You know…the Universal Law of energy.

You will notice then that, instead of being judgmental or critical about someone, you will send them a blessing instead. Actually it would be nice to bless everything and everyone you come in contact with. Bless and be thankful for your phone, your computer, your co-workers, sunlight, the rain, the plate you eat off of and the fork you use. Once you get used to living Thanksgiving Day every day, your whole life will explode into beauty.

Be in Thanksgiving
Be thankful for your eyes, for there are those who cannot see.
Be thankful for your ears, for there are those who cannot hear.
Be thankful for your voice, for there are those who cannot speak.
Be thankful for your heart, for there are those who know not love.

Did you ever think that for *every* negative thought you *ever* thought, for *every* negative word you *ever* spoke and for *every* negative action you *ever* took will have to be paid back with a positive thought, word, and action? Just think of how many of those unkind thoughts alone have been committed throughout our life. Much less all the unkind words and actions that we have taken. Stay conscious of your feeling world. Ask each day for forgiveness of all your past negative thoughts, words, and actions. It will not all release at once. So work on letting go of what you can each day. This will take daily conscious effort and with this, each day will become easier.

Call it karma, call it whatever, I see it as balancing life. We cannot expect to keep sending out negativity and not expect it to come back stronger than when we sent it. We will need to be ready with a positive counteraction to dissolve the negative when it returns. We have a long journey ahead of us, a long road back to the Light of God, but that is what we are all here for, to get back, to overcome these human tendencies of fear, greed, hatred, jealousy, disbelief, etc. These all can be overcome through forgiveness, letting go and through love. We may all not be taking the same road, but all roads with the right intention lead to God.

FOREST FIRE WITHIN

▼

What was the past, your past,
will be no more.

Now that we know that we want to be, in the light as opposed to being in the darkness, let us go a step further. Because of the negativity we want to work out of our being, there are a few proven methods that can help. Back when we were children and had all those seeds of negativity and false beliefs planted, just guess what that might look like today? Well, yes a forest has grown within us which means these are deep rooted and will take some work to get rid of.

Along with your thinking, speaking, and doing other works positively, you can see some of the trees of negativity falling to their demise. What we need is to start a forest fire (the only one you will deliberately start) within yourself. You can do this with visualization, with your imagination. We all know how strong that can be. Try this exercise and pretty soon, you will feel it working too.

Look within yourself and you will see the forest that has grown from the seeds of negativity that had been planted there long ago. You will see that some trees have fallen, but there will still be many, many strong trees still standing. Imagine a flame starting to burn throughout your forest. See this flame as a violet or purple color for this is the color of the highest level and vibration. It has the properties of transmutation, which is what we want to do with this negativity. This is the flame likened to the Burning Bush where Moses spoke to God.

Ask that all of your negative emotions and fears of the past be burned away. See your forest within dissolving down, keep letting it burn and burn until there are no more standing trees. They are all gone...dissolved. Once your negative forest is dissolved, acknowledge and know that these things of the past no longer serve you and you have released them forever.

This would be a good time to intentionally plant positive seeds into your subconscious. For instance, you can plant the seed of love, the seed of success, the seed of happiness, anything you want positive in your world. If you think about it, most everything in nature comes from a seed. Plant your seeds and nurture them and watch them grow into your world.

This is a very good exercise to do every week or every night if you wish. You want to make sure that no new seedlings of negativity start to sprout. I try to put myself daily into this cleansing chamber of violet God flame.

To keep myself on track, whenever I feel something negative trying to come up to me, I just tell it to "Dissolve, dissolve, dissolve, into the Light" over and over again until the negativity does in fact dissolve. I also state that I no longer need this negative idea. It no longer serves me so I send it away forever. Pluck it right out, pull the plug and it has no more power. It will have no power to affect, limit, or disturb you again.

You can also look right at the negativity or fear and give it the third degree. Ask it "Why are you still here?"…"Why do you continue to try and bother me?"…"Why do you think you can upset me?" Make *it* feel uncomfortable, and it will fly away and fast. This re-programs the subconscious to not bring it up again.

When you get deeper into releasing negative emotions and fears from your body, then you go through what I call a time of *processing*. It may be a day when you feel certain emotions and fears tugging at you because they know you are getting rid of them and they think you want them to stay. It may be a feeling of anxiety or sudden jolts of pain in certain areas of your body.

You can actually feel these emotions and fears leaving the body. Just like what is called butterflies in your stomach when you are nervous, or your heart sink when you feel let down. Watch what you feeling in your body when you are going through an emotion and that is where it is stored. These things are held in the body as well as the mind. They are real and it is a part of you that is *dying*. This is good, just nurture yourself and keep dissolving and focusing on God and it will just vanish.

After a time of processing and letting the negative parts of you die away, you will feel refreshed, renewed and stronger. Bear with it, for it is worth it. What was the past, your past, will be no more.

Essentially, what we are doing here is letting go of the old thoughts and patterns from our subconscious mind, which thereby releases the emotion from our body which is indeed a process.

It is important to understand that not only in the subconscious mind are these things stored but also in the bones, muscles, organs, and all the way down to the cellular level. We are multi-faceted beings and emotions of all levels are held within us everywhere. Releasing fears and negativity is only a first step to clearing the body to heal yourself. As you heal yourself, you are healing others. Everyone you come in contact with is affected at some level by how clear you are.

When I want to make a connection or if I feel a little out of balance, I tell myself to "Focus on God" over and over. This clears my mind and I put my focus in my heart while repeating "Focus on God." Staying in your heart space will keep your mind from wanting to chatter. This is how I have my continual communion with Him. This connection is always with the heart. By focusing and staying in your heart space, you will get your answers. While keeping your focus in the heart, go completely into the heart and feel it…feel God. Be still and listen through your heart for that is where the God inside you lives.

This is also where I go when my mind wants to daydream. Try to think more through your heart instead of your mind. The mind is where you hear the voice of confusion. The heart is pure. Ask to release this voice of confusion.

Focus on God
Open your heart
Let God do the rest.

At the end of every day, I look over my day and I feel the quirks of what thoughts, words, or actions I took that were not in positive alignment and I have my communion or confession with God to acknowledge what I did or said that was not quite right. After this, I feel so much better and the next time the same situation comes up, I stop in my tracks right away and regroup to a positive outcome.

Step toward re-programming your subconsious mind:

Quiet yourself and place your focus in your heart space. Ask that all pre-recorded cause, effect and record of any past misconceptions, seeming failures, untruths, disbeliefs, limits, pain, fear, despair, anything and all that you have in your subconscious mind that has held you back or caused limitation in any way, that this be released from your being and world now and forever. You no longer need to hold onto this information for it no longer serves you. So be it and so it is.

Fill your mind and body with golden light to replace the newly emptied space. This would be a good time to ask to have a stronger connection with your supraconscious mind. This will better enable you to process new information you come in contact with from this point on.

Matthew 6:6

But thou, when thou prayest, enter into thy closet, and when thou hast shut thy door, pray to thy Father which is in secret; and thy Father which seeth in secret shall reward thee openly.

Self-love results in healing yourself. Love is the real key to the universe. Yes, it is important to clear outside influences from your being, but the rest of it comes from you. From within. Only by going within to love ourselves will the true healing happen. As we embody self-love, it releases the God essence through us out into the world. You will reflect a new character, a sense of joy and energy that you have never felt before. The more you love yourself and being, the more your world will indeed change. You will look at life differently, see things and people in a new light. As I myself started doing this, I was surprised to see how people responded in a different way. Each day flows easier and you feel lighter in every way.

Leave behind worries and old thoughts. Focus on being clean, clear and in the present. Create your new world starting from within. There is no need to look for outward things or people to do this for you. You will keep searching on and on for years when it was right there inside *you* all the time. This is why some people are never happy or content and grasp for material things and different mates to fulfill their emptiness. They keep searching and are never content. When what they really needed to do, is look in the mirror and see the one they have been looking for. Only through going within, to love, can you find balance and contentment.

Love yourself. We are always so pre-occupied and wrapped up in our feelings of others that we forget that loving and nurturing our self is also important. Do not discount this. Self-love is the first step to healing yourself and your world. How do you expect others to love you when you do not love yourself?

As you cleanse and clear yourself, emotions that have been held in your organs, bones, muscles, and every part of you will start to dissolve and disappear. Do not allow negative thoughts or even put unhealthy food back into your body. What you allow in every day is settling somewhere in your being. Be conscious of this and let only positive constructive thoughts in. There is so much to release from our beings that we do not need to add to it on a daily basis. Use each day to release more and more. It all happens with the timing that you are allowing yourself to release. It does not happen all at once. It can be gradual.

I thought that I was getting pretty clear until I started my training as an energetic healer. I could then see how much that I was still holding on to. It is a daily process of focusing on connecting with your body...loving yourself and letting the old emotions and patterns release...they will just dissolve away.

It takes conscious awareness and effort to let go of past things in the subconscious mind. You do not need to analyze each emotion that is releasing. It is not necessary to deal with each issue. Look at it and let go immediately. Do not take time to think about it. Just look at it in neutrality and let it go.

It is a feeling of surrendering to God and the God essence inside you and just wanting to release everything that is holding you back from everything that you could have in your world. Surrender and allow yourself to be healed. It is only the last bit of darkness before the dawn.

For instance, (and talk to your body) release whatever may be holding you back from feeling happiness, love, joy or whatever fear is keeping your from stepping forward...let it go...we must keep stepping forward.

Self-love is the key to opening all the doors to the universe in your world. Open your heart. This taps into your own God essence. As you release and let go, your heart opens up like a flower. When it is fully opened, and you are projecting unconditional love, then everything will gravitate toward you, like bees to the nectar. Your business will soar and your personal life will be beautiful.

By continuing these examples, you will see things in your world getting ever brighter. Spread all of this outside of your world and throughout the world and there will be nothing left to nurture a negative seed or thought for it to grow. This is also a great service that you do for others and for the planet. Any positive energy you spread out can touch the lives of many.

This also reminds me of a night when I was up in the mountains for the weekend. I decided to start a fire in the fireplace. I worked for a good thirty minutes trying to start this fire with no success. All the time thinking to myself, how on earth do people start a forest fire so easily? I had been trying with newspaper, twigs, sticks, logs, many matches, and everything I had access to, short of throwing gasoline to it. It did light up but only lasted for probably three minutes. Finally, I just thought, oh well, no fire tonight and forgot about it.

Later that night, approximately four hours later, I noticed the smallest ember glowing in the fireplace. I was surprised that the little ember was still aglow, since the three minute fire was gone many hours ago. Some time later, I was awakened by the crackling of fire in the fireplace! Much to my amazement or should I say ablazement, I could not believe this fire was full force more than five hours after I tried to start it. In my attempt to go back to sleep, I was thinking to myself, so *that* is how a forest fire starts.

So you see, as long as you make the attempt to start your inner fire for clearing. As long as your intention is there, it may only start out as a little ember. Give it time and it will go full force to burn off all negativity fear and anything that is holding you back from moving forward.

HEAL THYSELF

▼

Forgiveness is one of the most healing things
You can do for yourself

As we have just seen how to start clearing the negativity from our being and world, it is now time to understand how we can heal ourselves. The subconscious mind holds the memory of the emotions and fears, and the body holds the emotions. These are held in the bones, muscles, organs and all the way down to our cellular level. Most of you have heard of the term cellular memory, which means that your cells have the emotion held in them. By using conscious means, we can help to release these fears and emotions which will set us free. It takes a great deal of conscious effort, but by being diligent and working every day with cleansing, clearing and releasing, you will feel lighter each day. The body responds to conscious direction.

Start with the intention of completely focusing on your body. As mentioned earlier, when you feel certain quirks or jolts of pain in certain areas of the body, this is where the emotion lies. Sometimes, all it takes is hearing someone mention a certain condition that will trigger the emotion to surface. When it does, be conscious of where you feel it. Work right away with telling your body to release the emotion, that it is alright and allow yourself to release. Allowing yourself to step forward is very important. Then visualize that area being filled with golden light to replace the empty space.

On a more direct level, sometimes working with a healer or one that understands energetic healing can greatly assist you in releasing. They can help you identify the emotions more readily. You may not be able to pick up some things by yourself right away without the assistance of a healer. This is because the past fear or emotion in your subconscious is keeping it deeply stored. You can release at what pace you are comfortable with. You will only let go of what you are ready to let go of and what your body feels safe of letting go at that time. Allow yourself to be healed.

Not only are these past emotions and fears held in the body but also are the effects of your present and everyday thoughts, feelings and words. Each time we focus our thought, have feelings, or speak words of criticism or negativity, it will have an effect not only in your body, but on your spiritual path as well. As we are cleaning, clearing and releasing from our body, we are also doing this for our spirit.

Just ask your higher self to help you flush out all pain, its cause, effect and records along with any distress from your thoughts and feelings in your body and world. Do this daily. Daily conscious effort is needed to allow your body and world to let go of what is no longer needed.

As I started this process, I first started by prayer and meditation to ask for any cause of dis-ease to be released. I wanted to release so badly whatever I had was holding on to. As this started to lift, I started working on releasing whatever may have happened in the past that I may not even be consciously aware of. It could be some fear or negative emotion that I did not remember.

By the time I was working on this, I had started my training as an energetic healer and learned about releasing everything that could be lodged anywhere in the body. I just kept asking and focusing every day, to release as much of the past that I can for that day and I was not going to allow it to control my future any longer. The more I kept affirming this, the more I could see this releasing. I was thinking cleansing and clearing all the time.

Each day, I looked forward to letting go of more. I came to the realization that along with trusting in God and connecting with body and mind…it all works together in creating your new life. The Divine plan.

As we all know, it is good to be conscious of eating healthy foods and exercising to keep our body healthy and in good condition. Good aerobic exercise helps the heart, clears the lungs, gets the blood circulating, and keeps the bones and muscles strong.

Remember that this body is where you live and you need to keep it healthy and strong. Once you start clearing emotions from the body, you will find that you will not be eating for emotional reasons as much. You will be more conscious of what you are putting into your body and not want to overindulge in unhealthy food. Although...I will probably never totally give up ice cream. Nor do we need to. We just need to have balance in our indulgences.

I know some people get squeamish when talking about colonics. A colonic is a flushing of the colon with water, done by a therapist trained in this field. Did you know that one colonic is worth 8-10 days of cleansing. I used to get one now and then after a juice fast, which I would do every spring, but I decided to really get into cleansing and did a series of colonics. Once you get your mind set for what you want to create, you seem compelled to go all the way. Anyway, once I started a series of these sessions, at about once a week at first, I was surprised to find my body going through emotional releasing. My colon therapist told me how other patients had gone through the same thing. Of course, then realizing how many emotions and what pain we must store in the intestines. This area is usually what feels like a punch in the stomach/solar plexus area when we get hit with bad news or a major emotional issue. A lot, and I mean a lot, of emotions are held in the stomach and intestines. I did find these sessions very helpful and therapeutic for physical and emotional releasing.

It is also important to bring our body back to a natural state. We have so many unnatural means that our bodies are subjected to daily. Most of which we consume that is full of chemicals. In most areas of the world, even the air we breathe is unhealthy and full of byproducts that we are inhaling. The water we drink, unless from a natural spring is chemically processed as well. All of this is going into our bodies daily. This is why it is very important to keep your body as healthy and possible through diet and exercise. I know a lot of this is unavoidable and sometimes necessary because of where we live and work.

However, just be conscious about your body. We have enough to deal with what we have stored inside emotionally through our thoughts, feelings and words. Let us not make it more difficult by having to deal with external causes. Be consciously aware and responsible of what you put into your body.

All forms of disease or discomfort are linked to some emotion or fear that we have. For example, I have found that, usually back pain is related to financial burden and feelings of responsibility, and/or any kind of burden that you carry. Chest pain is related to having your heart area closed down and not allowing love in. Stomach problems or digestive problems are related to worrying too much and letting things eat away at you. Usually pain in the hips and legs are from fear of stepping forward or getting ready to step forward.

Be aware of what your thoughts are and where you have discomfort or pain. Talk to your body and tell yourself that you want to release all causes and effects from this problem and just keep focusing on releasing. It will with conscious effort.

You can also every morning after getting up, do a little meditation, focus on God and simply ask for this day to be another step toward healing your body and your world. Ask for all levels of releasing whatever you can and what your body feels comfortable with releasing this day, and that you are ready for this. Just doing this simple step every day will result in a miracle of change for you.

As you continue to release more every day, you will find that your life flows with much more ease and miracles just happen for you. Beautify, perfecting and giving yourself health in body, mind, and spirit. You connect with a higher sense of knowing which definitely enriches your life to a healthy, happy world.

There is also an interesting fact that has been said and proven. The human body completely renews itself every eleven months. Meaning new cells, blood, skin, bones...everything. It has also been proven that through visualization and only seeing yourself the way you want to be, you can completely change your physical being every year. We only stay the same because that is the condition we expect. Just as we expect to age and therefore, we do. This could even make a change in our health. Through these mental pictures and affirming that this be so, your body will respond to your conscious direction. You can affirm that you no longer have some affliction or disease. This is how people have healed themselves from many things. This is also a form of believing and trusting in your self and in God.

I guess it might be easier to go to a monastery for a year so no outside influences would hinder you. But since we all cannot go to a sanctuary for a year, or take a year off, we can do this with continual daily conscious direction. Our mind controls our body. Put affirmations of what you want to be all over the house so you see them and repeat them every day. You could have a picture of yourself or of someone who equates to what you want to be. Keep the visualization and affirmations of how you want to be physically, whether it be a healthier back, younger skin, vibrant in every way, with no more disease or ailments. I think this would be a great year of transformation that we could all try.

Ten Commandments Revisited

▼

Most people, from any religious background have heard of the Ten Commandments. The verses in the Bible that tell of Moses going up to Mt. Sinai and speaking to God and who gave these commandments to mankind:

EXODUS 20:3-17

1   *Thou shalt have no other gods before me.*
     We are to believe that God is the only God. Some of the pagans made all sorts of gods and prayed to them instead of recognizing the true God.

2   *Thou shalt not make unto thee any graven image.*
     God did not want his children to make carved images of what they believed was God, or of anything else that they might worship. We are to believe in God the spiritual, not God the material. Some people "worship" their material possessions more than God. By this I mean money, houses, boats, all the toys.

3　*Thou shalt not take the name of the Lord thy God in vain.*

We are to respect God's name and not use it in context of emptiness or cursing.

4　*Remember the sabbath day, to keep it holy.*

God really wants us to take a day off. A day off from every kind of work. That might be hard for some of the retail stores, but if the only places open were churches and sanctuaries, just think how we could use that day for relaxation and celebration of God.

5.　*Honour thy father and thy mother.*

We must have respect for our parents. They brought us into this world. Bless them. Also honor God the Father-Mother.

6　*Thou shalt not kill.*

All life is sacred. We have no right to take a life God has given.

7　*Thou shalt not commit adultry.*

Most of us know what that means. Do not have impure intentions for another mans wife or another womans husband.

8　*Thou shalt not steal.*

This one is easy. Do not take what is not yours. If it is something that you have not worked for or bought with your own money...it is stealing. Could this also go for borrowing without asking?

9　*Thou shalt not bear false witness against thy neighbour*

This means lying. Do not speculate, gossip, make rumors or anything in that category without the truth behind it. Anyway, aren't there better things you can be doing?

10 *Thou shalt not covet thy neighbour*

We are not to have desires or long for another persons property or possessions. We are to remember that our material status means nothing to God. Especially when it comes out of ego. It is our spiritual status that is important.

These rules are quite easy. It is not so hard to lead a spiritual life. Why do so many people turn away?

MAKING IT ALL FIT

▼

Thy kingdom come. Thy will
Be done in earth, as it is in heaven.
Matthew 6:10

Whether you have been on your spiritual path for many years or whether this is the first book that you have read about this subject, there is no better time than now to start. We were born to our own self, so we have our own self to set upon this journey. Everyone that you know is going at whatever pace they are comfortable with. Even someone that does not seem to care about their own spirituality, it is all right. They are moving at the pace that is right for them. Sooner or later they will start to see. Do not feel responsible if others are not interested in their spiritual journey or what you are doing for your spiritual journey. This is because it is your *own* journey to take to get *yourself* through. It is *your* commitment to get *yourself* back to God.

I know for I have taken most of my steps alone. I have been on this path for most of my life and I know that I still have a long way to go.

Getting to the point that you are willing to surrender everything to get back to God is a real freeing feeling. I have been willing to not care so much about material possessions. When you let go of material things or your attachment to them, then the even greater gifts from God come to you. The key is to not be attached to them.

Take responsibility for your own life. It is you who is responsible for yourself and not another human. This is between you and God-the Divine. Your responsibility.

Find happiness within yourself, not from outer acquirements or depend on others to be the source of your happiness. True happiness comes from connecting to the God within. Love yourself.

Step out of the past and close the door. Step forward into the Divine path...the Divine plan. Illuminate your life. Become enlightened. Have the knowing of I AM. Set yourself free. Only you can do this for yourself.

We carry both the beautiful light of God conscious awareness and the human denseness of the physical...the senses...the emotions and how we interpret every thought and feeling. It can be a challenge to balance all the elements. We can get caught up in observing others with their drama and how they live through themselves. We start to act the same as though we need the drama too.

Much like the monkey see, monkey do syndrome. It takes conscious effort to slow down and filter our thoughts and feelings. We do not have to be like everyone else. We are all unique. Find your own uniqueness and love that part of you. Love being unique. Also, love every part of yourself.

Ultimately, we are all on the same journey, so lets take each breath, each minute, each hour and day at a time.

Live very consciously and be focused in the present. Be aware of what your are thinking, speaking and doing. This makes **all** the difference in the world…in your world. It does not have to be anybody else's world, just *yours*. Clear yourself of negative thoughts, negative words and negative actions. Do not listen to others that want this in their lives. You do not have to participate in gossip sessions or putting out anything negative just because someone else is. If you do something that is not of the best intentions, just stop and reflect on the circumstances. Take some time for introspection and you will realize within yourself what is the *right* thing to do. Give all your fears and worries up to God. Surrender it up to Him. He will take care of this for you.

As you do this, each day becomes easier. You will be challenged by negativity and your ego. You just need to have the will to stand up to it and the negativity will no longer exist. Balance yourself. Cleanse, clear, heal, and love yourself. Stand strong on your own and set the example. Claim this truth and live by it. What thoughts, words or actions do you want to live through?

Remember as you go through these steps:
Focus on God, open your heart, let God do the rest.
Let go of the fear and step through the doorway.
Take the passage into the rest of your life.

As you keep working with these examples that have been outlined, you will start to see all of your puzzle pieces fitting into your world easily. As you are willing to let go of your fears that have kept you prisoner for so many years, then many doors open for you. Recognize that you are the creator of your own world. You have created your reality and you are the only one to change it. Allow yourself to be healed and open to allowing in God's gifts. Then accept it and then expect it. Just when you think you have totally surrendered to God, then it is time to surrender some more. Each time your load lightens. As you are truly wanting to do God's will, when this is the utmost desire, then you will be completely amazed at what you can accomplish and truly Love your Life.

Daily Reminders

You are the only one creating your world.

Only you can take the steps for yourself.

Allow God to assist you.

Allow yourself to let go of the past and step onto your Divine path.

Release at least one thing from your past emotional feeling world every day.

Do not allow any negative thought to affect you. Pull the plug to its power.

Let go of fear, it has no power.

Focus on God, Open your heart, Let God do the rest.

Let go of the fear and step through the doorway.

Take the passage into the rest of your life.

AFTERWORD

▼

Now that you have read *Love You Life*, you can now get started on creating your own new world and a life that you will love and that is waiting for you.

You can read this book over and over again. Each time you read it, you will pick up something new or different. Keep a copy at your bedside and read out of this book before retiring in the evening and, when getting up in the morning. This will help end your day and start your new day with a fresh positive outlook.

May God's blessings pour forth into your world and entire life always.

ABOUT THE AUTHOR

▼

A seeker of the truth and spiritual path. Sharing in her own life experiences and insights to assist others to find their own true path.